Unit 6

HOUGHTON MIFFLIN HARCOURT
School Publishers

Contents

Bears

by Anne Miranda

What things do bears like? Just look and see!

Bears like eating. This black bear
is sitting up in a tree. It is getting
nuts. It grabbed them and ate them.
It likes eating nuts!

Bears like fishing. Fishing is best when streams are filled with fish. Fast swimming fish race past this bear. They are racing up stream.

Bears like swimming. It is a thrill
to see this big, white bear swimming
in the sea! It is bobbing up and
down in the waves like floating ice.
It swims toward the ice.

This bear has an itch. He likes scratching. He is rubbing his back on that tree. He looks as if he is grinning. He must have found just the spot to scratch.

This bear likes napping. It can
sleep well even during the day. It will
wake up and go trotting off to look
for food. It will eat and nap again.
This bear likes napping a lot.

This bear likes digging. It has been digging a den. It will line its den with branches and grass. Grass makes a soft mattress. It will be a nice bed to nap in.

9

This bear likes sleeping at night with the moon shining above. It stretched and nodded off. Sleep well, bear! Sleep well!

Hiding and Seeking

by Lance Langley
illustrated by Dominic Catalano

The kits liked their first grade
teacher, Miss Fox. Miss Fox liked
them, and she liked playing games.
She was fun!

At playtime, the kits begged for
a game of Hide and Seek. Miss Fox
was IT. Miss Fox counted to ten.
Her class hid while she counted.

Red was hiding in a good place, but he did not sit still. He wagged his tail. Miss Fox spotted Red. She tagged him. Red was out.

Meg was hiding in this very good place, but her ears jutted out. Miss Fox spotted Meg. She tagged her. Meg was out.

Blaze was hiding in a good place,
but he clapped and hummed. Miss
Fox spotted Blaze. She tagged him.
Blaze was out.

Jill was hiding in a good place.
She hid in a tree above Miss Fox.
Miss Fox looked and looked but she
didn't see Jill. Jill smiled.

Miss Fox hunted up and down for Jill. Jill had fun fooling Miss Fox. Jill's laughs made Jill's tree shake. Miss Fox saw it shaking.

Miss Fox spotted Jill at last! Miss
Fox tagged her. Jill was out. Jill
was good at hiding, but Miss Fox was
great at seeking!

Henry and Dad Go Camping

by Ting Biderman
illustrated by Stacey Schuett

Dad put up the tent. Henry hurried to pump up the beds. Dad was sleepy, but Henry gazed up at the stars.

Then Henry sat up surprised.
What was that hissing sound?   Henry
poked his dad and woke him up.

"What's hissing?" Dad asked.

"It's creepy," said Henry. "It must be snakes!"

"Snakes?" asked Dad. "Maybe."

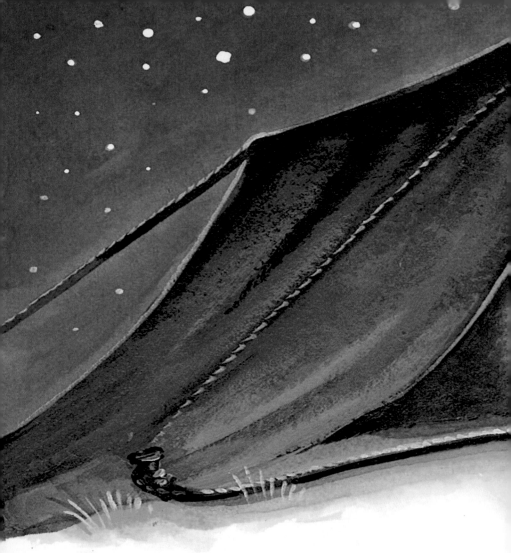

Dad shined a light toward
the grass.

"I can see something that's long
and thin like a snake," Dad said.
"Is it hissing?" asked Henry.

"No," Dad said. "It's not hissing.
It's just a rope."

"The hissing hasn't stopped!
What can it be?" Henry asked.

Dad flashed the light inside the tent.

"Look at your bed, Henry," said Dad. "It's getting as flat as a pancake. Your leaky bed is hissing, not snakes."

Henry felt silly but safe. He
felt sleepy, too. He went to sleep
as his flat bed hissed its last hiss.

Speedy and Chase

by Christopher K. Lyne
illustrated by Rick Stromoski

It was sunny but not too hot. It was a good day for a race. Goats, pigs, and cows lined up in the field. They would get a good look.

Chase looked at Speedy. Chase studied him. Speedy hopped in place. Chase hoped he could keep up with Speedy. Was Speedy as speedy as he looked?

"I plan on winning this race!"
shouted Speedy.

"You seem fast," said Chase.

"Yes!" Speedy grinned. "Fast
and planning on winning. It will be
easy!"

"Get ready. Go!" yelled Sheep.
Speedy zoomed past clapping
fans. Speedy really was speedy!
Chase jogged past them at his own
slow pace.

Speedy took the lead. "Chase can't catch up," Speedy bragged. "I feel a bit sleepy. I will win even if I take a nap!"

He flopped down and napped.

Speedy was still napping when
Chase jogged by. He was running at
his own slow pace. He was smiling,
too.

Chase pushed on toward the finish line. Chase didn't give up. He kept on going. Fans clapped and yelled. Speedy woke up surprised!

Speedy had planned on winning, but Chase was first. Chase was the winner!

The Three Races

by Madeleine Jeffries

illustrated by Amanda Harvey

Fran had her box of cars. She
and Ken each chose two racecars.

Ken picked a slick red racecar.
Fran picked next. She chose a much
bigger blue car. Fran hoped it was
faster, too. Speedier cars win!

Then Ken picked a racecar with black stripes. Fran picked next. Fran picked a green car. It was nicer and had fatter wheels than Ken's.

In the first race, Fran's bigger
blue car raced Ken's slick red car.
Ken and Fran lined them up at the
top of the hill.

Fran's car zipped faster than
Ken's. Ken's car was much slower.
Fran's car raced fast enough to win.
That made Fran happy.

In the next race, Ken's striped car
raced Fran's green car. This time,
Ken's car zoomed faster. It was fast
enough to win. It made Ken happy.

Ken and Fran had one last race.
Fran's speedy blue car raced Ken's
fast striped car.

Which car would be faster?

The cars raced at the same speed.
Fran's car was not faster. Ken's car
was not faster. That made Fran and
Ken happy, too!

Seed Sisters

by Anne Miranda
illustrated by Janet Pedersen

It is spring. Liz and Rose are
shopping for seeds. Liz and Rose
always plant seeds in the spring.

Rose picks a smaller pack of
seeds. Liz's pack is much bigger.
Liz and Rose go back home to plant
the seeds that they just got.

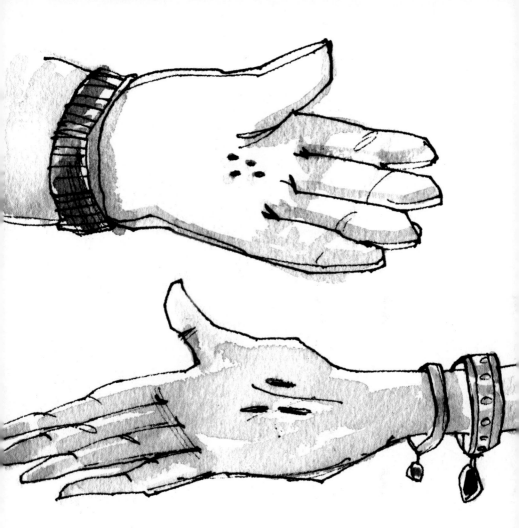

Liz and Rose see that the seeds in each pack are different. Rose's seeds are much smaller and rounder. Liz's seeds are much longer and flatter.

Liz and Rose dig. Liz digs faster
than Rose. Liz plants her seeds first.
Rose digs slower than Liz. Rose
plants her seeds last.

The seeds sprout. Liz's seeds
sprout quicker. Rose's seeds are
slower to sprout. Liz and Rose rake
and weed their backyard plot once.

All spring the plants grow. They grow bigger and bigger and bigger each day. Liz's plants are different from Rose's.

Liz's plants grow higher than
Rose's plants. Rose's are shorter.
Rose and Liz tell stories as they
wait for the plant buds to open!

The plants are in bloom. How
nice the backyard looks! Rose and
Liz think their yard is the nicest yard
in town!

The Fox and the Grapes

retold by Lindsey Pare
illustrated by Jeff Mack

Digger Fox is always happy to
see Gram. Gram has a big back
porch. Digger is happiest there.
Grapes grow near that porch.

51

Gram brings lunch. She brings
the reddest apples Digger has
ever seen. He likes grapes better,
but the grapes aren't ripe yet.

Gram goes inside. Digger has a plan. He jiggles the benches closer to the grapes. He just has to have a grape!

Digger jiggles himself up. He
reaches for the biggest bunch of
grapes. He wiggles up, up, up.
Then Digger tumbles down. Gram
catches him.

Gram cuddles Digger and tells him, "You must be the luckiest little fox ever. I got here just in time."

"Can't I eat one grape, Gram?" asks Digger.

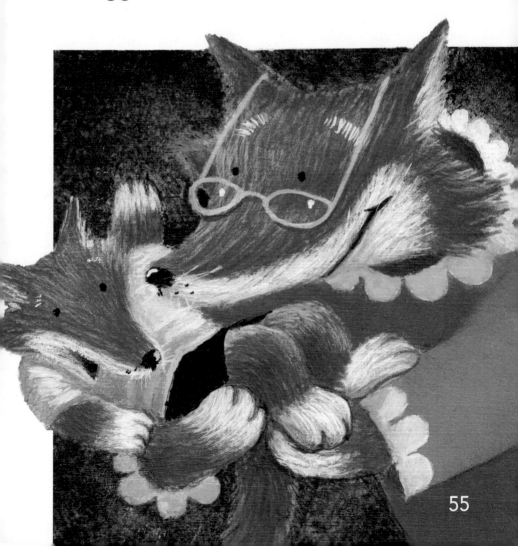

Gram reaches for a grape and
hands it to Digger. He tastes it.

"Yuck," he grumbles. "It tastes like a pickle!"

"Yes," winks Gram. "The grapes aren't ripe yet. Next time, trust me."

Digger puts the benches back in place. Gram will ask Digger back when the grapes get ripe. Digger can't wait! Those grapes are much tastier when they are ripe!

Jingle, Jangle, and Jiggle

by Jose Pitkin

illustrated by Judy Stead

Jingle, Jangle, and Jiggle are
pals. Jingle is the shortest. Jiggle is
the biggest. Jangle is in the middle.

Jingle, Jangle, and Jiggle are
clowns. Clowns make us chuckle and
giggle. They always dress in funny
hats and pants. They put on funny
noses.

Jiggle has the longest nose. It makes a loud honking sound. Now it is missing! Where can it be? It is a puzzle. Jiggle must get it back!

Jiggle looks inside Jangle's boots.
He looks inside Jingle's hat.   Jiggle
does not see his nose.   He starts
to grumble.

Jiggle looks in high places. Jingle
looks in low places. Silly Jangle looks
in a popcorn box! Jiggle's nose is still
missing.

Jiggle sobs and sniffles. "I need
my nose," he mumbles. Then a
blue bird comes near. Jiggle's nose
dangles from the bird's beak!

Jiggle jumps up. The bird zooms high. Jiggle cannot catch it. Then the bird dips low. Jiggle tackles that bird. He snatches his nose back!

Jiggle puts on his nose. He gives
it the biggest, loudest, silliest honk he
can! Then Jingle, Jangle, and Jiggle
take a bow.

Sally Jane and Beth Ann

by James McKinley
illustrated by Tom Leonard

Sally Jane was a large brown bat.
She spent much of her time hanging
by her feet in her safe, dark cave.

At night, Sally Jane liked to
fly across the sky. She could hear
sounds from far away. Her good
hearing helped her catch bugs.

Last night, Sally Jane heard an
odd sound. She saw a bat that
needed help. It was Beth Ann.

"My wing is snagged in this net,"
Beth Ann cried.

"I will try to get you out," Sally
Jane said with a bright smile.

Sally Jane gave it her best try.
She tugged and bit at the net. At
last, Beth Ann got free!

"Let's fly," said Sally Jane.

"I can't fly," groaned Beth Ann.
"My wing is still stiff."

"My, my, so it is," sighed Sally
Jane. "Let me try to pick you up. I
can fly you back to my cave."

"You can lift me!" cried Beth Ann.

"I am strong," boasted Sally Jane.

"Let's go then!" said Beth Ann.

Sally Jane held Beth Ann tight
and took flight.

Sally Jane flew high across the
sky. Beth Ann was in her grasp. They
landed in the cave. Beth Ann thanked
Sally Jane. Sally Jane was happy to
help her new buddy, Beth Ann.

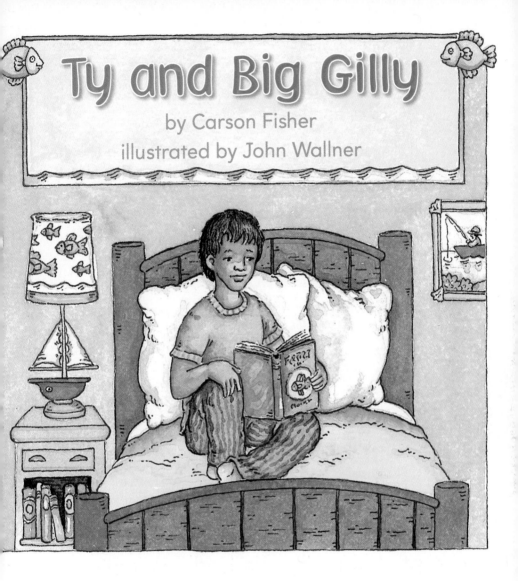

Ty and Big Gilly

by Carson Fisher

illustrated by John Wallner

Ty had a hobby that made him happy. His hobby was fishing. Ty liked fishing.

Ty had a large fishing box. He
kept it right by his bed. It was filled
with hooks, jelly bugs, and all sorts
of fishing stuff. It had a fly that his
dad had made.

One bright, sunny day, Ty and his
dad went fishing. Ty had his fishing
box, rod, and reel. He and Dad
hiked to Sand Lake.

Ty sat under the pale blue sky as he baited his hook. He used a jelly bug. Ty closed his fishing box lid. Ty tried to keep the box neat and clean.

Ty threw back his line. He let it
fly high across the lake. His jelly bug
landed with a plop! Dad cast his
line. Ty and Dad waited.

Then Ty had a bite! Ty had to
reel it in. He gave it his best try.
The fish was fighting hard. Then the
fish on his line jumped up and out of
the water. It was big!

It jumped a second time. What a
sight! It was Big Gilly! Big Gilly had
a big head. Its tail snapped back
and forth. "That's the biggest fish in
Sand Lake," Dad cried out.

Ty grabbed Big Gilly and took out
the hook. He let Big Gilly go. Big
Gilly swam off, still king of Sand Lake.
Dad winked at Ty. He was glad Ty
let Big Gilly go.

Bird Watching

by Rebecca McDermott

This is a large bird. Three large eggs can fit in its nest. That huge nest is quite a sight!

This bird has a long bill. It flies low across the sea. It scoops up a lot of fish in that long bill!

Look at this bird's long, bright tail!
It looks like a fan. Its tail is shiniest
in sunlight. This bird is fun to see.

This hawk can take flight high across the sky. Then it can dive down in a flash. It can fly faster than a racecar can race!

Which bird is the fastest
swimmer? Few birds swim, but
this one can zoom right by. It
looks like it is flying in water!

This bird is the biggest and the strongest. One of its eggs is as big as 24 hen's eggs. It is the fastest runner, too!

This bird is not big. Its
nest is not big. Its eggs are
not big. Keep your eyes open
if you want to spy this bird!

What can this bird do best?
It sings the sweetest songs.
Hush.   You might hear it!

Benches

by Jillian Raymundo

illustrated by Elizabeth Sayles

Benches! Benches! Benches! See
them in cities. See them in towns.
See them in parks. See them at
beaches. Benches! Benches!

Benches are like outside couches.
They are good places to sit. Kids
sit on benches in yards and parks.
Buddies can sit side by side and chat.

Dogs and puppies go out on
leashes. Grown-ups, kids, and pets
sit on benches. Benches are good for
sitting and resting.

Kids eat lunch on benches.
Many kids have lunchboxes. When
lunchtime is over the kids might sit
and rest on benches. Then they
might play ball or jump rope.

Kids read books on benches. Kids read the funnies and comics, too. Kids read on benches when it is sunny and bright. When it rains, benches are not good places for reading.

Kids play games on benches.
Some kids are winners. Some kids
don't win. Still, kids like playing
games outside.

Moms, dads, and kids sit on
benches at beaches. This dad likes
to watch the sea flow in and out.
What a sight!

Benches for you and benches for me,
on city streets or at the sea!
I should sit and you should, too,
on benches at parks or at the zoo!

Quiz Game

by Cindy Wahl

This book has a quick quiz. Each page took me a minute. I'm hopeful that you'll like this book.

Which animal can sing sweetly?
Which can purr softly? Which can
growl loudly? Which can make
a squeaky sound?

Which animal can zip by quickly?
Which will go by slowly? Which can
wiggle by in a zigzag path? Which
can go by in a leap?

Which animal has long, helpful
claws? Which has a big hump?
Which can be stinky? Which looks
spotty?

Which fish looks like a snake?
Which has three white stripes? Which
has five black stripes? Which has
more than six legs?

Which animal has a shell? Which animals are furry? Which is a dog? Which is a cat? Which is the biggest?

Which bird can fly? Which can
swim in icy water? Which has bright
feathers? Which has long legs?

Did you like this quick quiz? Was
it fun? Do you have an idea for a
new quiz?

Jack and the Beans

by Anthony Swede
illustrated by Holli Conger

Jack and Jill had a big plot of land and a nice fat cow, but Jack and Jill did not have much food. Jack and Jill ate their last handful of oatmeal.

Jack had an idea. He took his nice fat cow to town. He thought he could sell his cow and get food.

Jack was in town a long, long time. Jill did not feel happy.

At last, Jack came back with a
bagful of beans. Jack looked joyful.
He felt hopeful, but Jill was still
upset. Jack had traded his nice fat
cow for that bagful of silly beans!

That bagful of beans could not
feed them for long. Then Jill listened
to Jack's idea. Jill liked it a lot.
She gladly helped Jack with his plan.

Jack and Jill quickly got spades
and rakes. Jack and Jill dug up some
rows on their plot of land. Jack and
Jill planted Jack's beans in long rows.

Then Jack and Jill went down the hill to fetch a pail of water. Jack and Jill drenched the dry black soil one cupful at a time. Jack and Jill waited hopefully.

Soon, the beans sprouted. Jack
and Jill were happy to see those
beautiful green sprouts in that black
soil. They felt hopeful as those bean
plants grew and grew and grew.

Jack and Jill picked bagful after bagful of beans. Those beans would last them a long, long time. Jack and Jill were thankful that Jack had such a good idea.

Ruth's Day

by Brady Frances
illustrated by Hideko Takahashi

Buzz! The clock buzzed loudly.
Ruth slowly got out of bed.
Ruth stretched and yawned.
She was still sleepy.

115

Ruth sat at the table. She ate her Crunchy Pops quickly. She did not like to let them get squishy or soggy.

It was chilly, so Ruth got dressed
quickly. Her bus came down the road
slowly. Ruth was a little late.

The bus stopped and beeped.
Ruth caught the bus just in time.
She had not missed the bus. She
felt happy.

Ruth sat with Edith. Edith smiled
sweetly. Ruth smiled back. It was
fun to sit with Edith. Ruth felt happy.

"Knock, knock," said Edith.

"I know that joke," said Ruth.
"It's funny."

"It's goofy," said Edith.

Ruth and Edith grinned. The bus went on slowly. At last, it got to the school.

Ruth and Edith sat in class.
Edith had left her math book at
home. Ruth let Edith use hers.
Edith was grateful.

Edith smiled and said, "I'm
happy to have your friendship,
Ruth." Ruth felt happy, too.

When Ruth got home, Mom
gave her a big hug. Ruth felt so
happy. She had a great day!

Stew for Peg

by Frank Fenn

illustrated by Laurie Hamilton

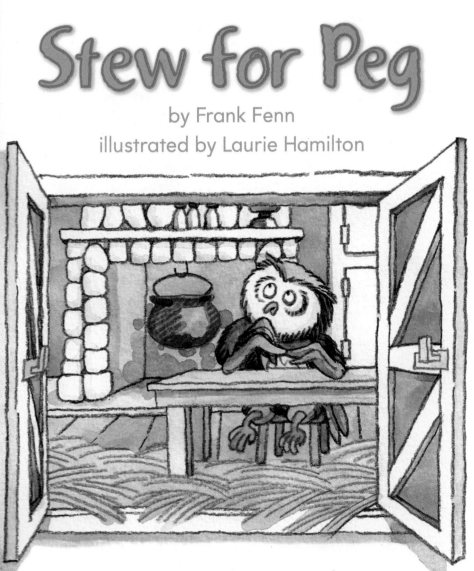

Jo Owl sat in her cozy home.
It was Peg Pig's birthday. Jo had
an idea.

"Peg likes stew," hooted Jo. "I will make a big pot of stew for Peg."

Jo was not able to make stew on her own. She didn't know how. She put a big pot of water in her cart. She went to ask for help.

Toby was helpful. He put a cupful
of red stuff in the pot.

"This will make Peg's stew really
yummy," Toby quacked loudly.

"Thanks, Toby!" hooted Jo.

Lulu was helpful. She put a
handful of green leaves in the pot.
   "This will make Peg's stew really
yummy," Lulu chattered quickly.
   "Thanks, Lulu!" hooted Jo.

Jo went back home. Hugo
came by.

"Hi," said Hugo. "What is
in that pot?"

"It's really yummy stew for
Peg," hooted Jo.

"Is it hot?" asked Hugo.

"Really yummy stew must be hot."

Hugo helped Jo heat it up.

"Thanks, Hugo!" hooted Jo.

"This stew smells yummy!"

Jo went to Peg's with her stew.

"What a treat!" squealed Peg.
"How did you make such yummy
stew, Jo?"

"I had some help," hooted Jo.

"Thank you!" squealed happy
Peg. "Thank you all for your
friendship! And thank you for
this really yummy stew!"

Amy Ant

by Denise Dinkleman
illustrated by Jon Goodell

Amy Ant wakes up. It has been a long, sleepy winter. Now winter is over. It is time to leave her cozy bed.

Amy makes her way up to the field. It is sunny. How good that sunshine feels! Spring has come at last.

Flowers are blooming. Amy
decides to pick some. She sniffs the
roses. She loves that smell the most.
It reminds her of sunny days.

When her backpack is full, Amy
returns home. The sweet smell of
roses fills each room. Amy is so
happy she hums a tune. Soon music
fills each room, too.

One day, Amy sees a blue flower.
She did not see it before. She crawls
up for a better look. Amy slips!
Down, down, she slides. She is not
able to get out.

Amy shouts for help. A flying
mantis hears her. He flies into the
flower and saves Amy!

Amy thanks him and thanks him!
He tells her that his name is Rupert.

"You're as brave as a tiger!" Amy tells him.

After that, Amy and Rupert meet every day. They take walks and look at flowers. They talk and have fun.

Summer is ending. Winter will
soon be on its way. Amy has to go
back down into her home. She waves
at Rupert. She is not sad. She will
see him in the sunshine next spring!

Julie and Jason

by Mason Sciele
illustrated by France Brassard

Julie has a pet rabbit named
Jason. Jason has black and white
fur. He sleeps in a cozy rabbit hutch
on Julie's back porch. Julie got Jason
when he was a baby.

Julie feeds Jason rabbit pellets
and hay. Jason likes his dinner. He
can sit up and behave like a dog.
After he eats, Jason can behave like
a cat. He curls up on Julie's lap.

Each day, Julie takes Jason out of
his hutch. Jason likes to play "Hide
and Seek." Jason hides and Julie
seeks. Jason sits still and silent as
Julie hunts for him.

One day, Julie's brothers took
Jason with them on a picnic. They
did not see Jason hop off beyond the
picnic table.

It was time for Julie to play with
Jason. Jason was not in his hutch or
on the porch. Julie looked all over
the house. She even looked behind
the drapes. Julie was upset. She
couldn't believe Jason was missing!

Julie asked her brothers if they had seen Jason. Julie's brothers were sorry they had let Jason hop away. Then everyone looked for Jason outside.

No one was able to find Jason.
Julie was sad. Then she had an idea.
Was Jason playing "Hide and Seek"?
She looked in places Jason had
hidden before.

Julie spotted Jason by a big
plant. She smiled. Jason saw Julie
and hopped out. Julie was so happy!
Her brothers were happy, too.

Home at Last

by Forest Von Gront

illustrated by Kristin Barr

Tony and his family were in
their new home. Tony was
happy. Everyone was happy!

Dad repainted Tony's new bedroom. Tony helped. Dad let Tony decide which paint he liked. Tony was glad he chose blue.

Dad unwrapped three new lights.
He replaced the old lights. Tony's
new room looked much brighter.

Then the van came at noon.
The workers quickly unloaded the
van. Everyone helped put things
where they belonged.

Tony unpacked his books. He and Mom unpacked sheets and made his bed. Before long, the room started to look cozy.

Tony found his box of toys. Then
his bedroom began to look like home.
It was nice to settle in so quickly.

Tony helped unpack dishes,
pots, and pans. Dad set up a table.
Mom, Dad, and Tony ate their first
meal in their new home.

The long day was over. There was still a lot to do, but it felt like home. Tony loved it! So did Mom and Dad.

Soccer

by Tia Yushi

illustrated by Linda Solovic

Many people believe soccer
is the best sport. Most boys and
girls play soccer.

Each player is dressed for soccer.
This coach and everyone on his team
have the same kind of shirt. This
team chose red shirts with dots. This
is the red team.

This coach and her team decided
on stripes. This is the blue team.
Their shirts look unlike the red team's
shirts. These players are putting on
long socks over shin pads.

Soccer teams need good skills.
At first, team players may be
unskilled at using only their feet on
the field. The more teams play, the
more skillful players get.

Soccer is a fast game. Soccer
teams must behave safely. It is
unsafe and unkind to bump into
players. It is a coach's job to teach
and remind players to play safely.

Each team's job is to score goals. Blue team players try to kick the ball into the red team's goal. Each team has a goalkeeper. The red team's goalkeeper tries to stop the blue team's players from making goals.

A goalkeeper is the only player
who can pick up the ball. He or she
can catch it and keep it out of the
goal. Goalkeepers must react fast
and stop goals.

When the game ends, players say
"Good job!" no matter who wins.
Kids have fun replaying soccer games
by telling and retelling plays their
team made.

Word Lists

Bears

Decodable Words
Target Skill: Inflections *-ed*, *-ing* (CVC*e*, CVC)

bobbing, digging, getting, grabbed, grinning, napping, nodded, racing, rubbing, sitting, shining, swimming, trotting

Previously Taught Skills
an, and, as, at, ate, back, be, bed, best, big, black, branches, can, day, den, down, during, eat, eating, fast, filled, fish, fishing, floating, food, for, found, go, grass, has, he, his, ice, if, in, is, it, itch, its, just, like, likes, line, look, looks, lot, makes, mattress, moon, must, nap, nice, nuts, off, on, past, race, scratch, scratching, sea, see, sleep, sleeping, soft, spot, stream, streams, stretched, swims, that, them, things, this, thrill, tree, up, wake, waves, well, when, white, will, with

High-Frequency Words
New

above, bear, bears, even, toward

Previously Taught

a, again, are, been, do, have, night, the, they, to, what

163

Hiding and Seeking

Decodable Words

Target Skill: Inflections *-ed*, *-ing* (CVC*e*, CVC)

begged, clapped, hiding, hummed, jutted, liked, shaking, smiled, spotted, tagged, wagged

Previously Taught Skills

and, at, Blaze, but, class, counted, did, didn't, down, ears, first, fooling, for, Fox, fun, game, games, good, grade, had, he, her, hid, hide, him, his, hunted, in, it, Jill, Jill's, kits, last, looked, made, Meg, Miss, not, out, place, playing, playtime, Red, saw, see, seek, seeking, shake, she, sit, still, tail, ten, them, this, tree, up, while

High-Frequency Words

New

above, teacher

Previously Taught

a, great, laughs, the, their, to, very, was

Henry and Dad Go Camping   page 19

Decodable Words
Target Skill: Long *e* Spelling Patterns
y, ie
creepy, Henry, hurried, leaky, silly,
sleepy

Target Skill: Base Words/Inflections
-ed, -ing (CVC*e*, CVC)
gazed, getting, poked, shined, stopped,
surprised

Previously Taught Skills
and, as, asked, at, be, bed, beds, but,
can, Dad, felt, flashed, flat, grass,
hasn't, he, him, his, hiss, hissed,
hissing, inside, is, it, its, it's, just, last,
like, long, look, maybe, must, no, not,
pancake, pump, rope, safe, sat, see,
sleep, snake, snakes, sound, stars, tent,
that, that's, then, thin, too, up, went,
woke

High-Frequency Words
New
surprised, toward

Previously Taught
a, I, light, put, said,
something, the, to, was,
what, what's, your

Speedy and Chase

Decodable Words

Target Skill: Long *e* Patterns *y*, *ie*
easy, field, ready, really, sleepy, Speedy, studied, sunny

Target Skill: Inflections *-ed*, *-ing* (CVC*e*, CVC)
bragged, clapped, clapping, flopped, grinned, hoped, hopped, jogged, lined, napped, napping, planned, planning, running, smiling, winning

Previously Taught Skills
and, as, at, be, bit, but, can't, catch, Chase, cows, day, didn't, down, fans, fast, feel, finish, first, for, get, go, goats, going, good, had, he, him, his, hot, if, in, it, keep, kept, lead, line, look, looked, nap, not, on, own, pace, past, pigs, place, plan, race, seem, Sheep, shouted, slow, still, take, them, this, too, took, up, when, will, win, winner, with, woke, yelled, yes, you, zoomed

High-Frequency Words

New
even, pushed, studied, surprised, toward

Previously Taught
a, by, could, give, I, said, the, they, was, would

The Three Races

page 35

Decodable Words
Target Skill: Inflections *-er, -est*
bigger, faster, fatter, nicer, slower, speedier

Previously Taught Skills
and, at, be, black, blue, box, car, cars, chose, each, fast, first, Fran, Fran's, green, had, happy, her, hill, hoped, in, it, Ken, Ken's, last, lined, made, much, next, not, picked, race, racecar, racecars, raced, red, same, she, slick, speed, speedy, striped, stripes, than, that, them, then, this, time, too, top, up, wheels, which, win, with, zipped, zoomed

High-Frequency Words
New
enough, happy

Previously Taught
a, of, one, the, to, two, was, would

Seed Sisters

page 43

Decodable Words
Target Skill: Inflections *-er*, *-est*
bigger, faster, flatter, longer, nicest,
quicker, rounder, shorter, slower

Previously Taught Skills
and, as, back, backyard, bloom, buds,
day, dig, digs, each, first, for, from, go,
got, grow, her, home, how, in, is, it,
just, last, Liz, Liz's, looks, much, nice,
pack, picks, plant, plants, plot, rake,
Rose, Rose's, see, seeds, shopping,
spring, sprout, stories, tell, than, that,
think, town, wait, weed, yard

High-Frequency Words
New
always, different, higher,
once, stories

Previously Taught
a, all, are, of, open, smaller,
the, their, they, to

LESSON 27

The Fox and the Grapes

page 51

Decodable Words

Target Skill: Syllable -_le
apples, cuddles, grumbles, jiggles, little, pickle, tumbles, wiggles

Target Skill: Inflections -*er*, -*est*
biggest, closer, Digger, happiest, luckiest, reddest, tastier

Previously Taught Skills
and, ask, asks, back, be, benches, better, big, brings, bunch, but, can't, catches, down, eat, ever, for, fox, get, got, Gram, grape, grapes, grow, hands, happy, has, he, him, himself, in, inside, is, it, just, like, likes, lunch, me, much, must, next, place, plan, porch, reaches, ripe, see, seen, she, tastes, tells, that, then, those, time, trust, up, wait, when, will, winks, yes, yet, you, yuck

High-Frequency Words

New
always, happy, near

Previously Taught
a, are, aren't, goes, have, here, I, of, one, puts, the, there, they, to

Jingle, Jangle, and Jiggle

page 59

Decodable Words

Target Skill: Syllable -_le_
chuckle, dangles, giggle, grumble,
Jangle, Jangle's, Jiggle, Jiggle's, Jingle,
Jingle's, middle, mumbles, puzzle,
sniffles, tackles

Target Skill: Inflections -*er*, -*est*
biggest, longest, loudest, shortest,
silliest

Previously Taught Skills
and, back, be, beak, bird, bird's, blue,
boots, bow, box, can, cannot, catch,
clowns, dips, dress, from, funny, get,
has, hat, hats, he, his, honk, honking,
in, inside, is, it, jumps, looks, loud, low,
make, makes, missing, must, need,
nose, noses, not, now, on, pals, pants,
places, popcorn, see, silly, snatches,
sobs, sound, starts, still, take, that, then,
up, us, zooms

High-Frequency Words

New
always, high, near

Previously Taught
a, are, comes, does, gives, I,
my, put, puts, the, they, to,
where

Sally Jane and Beth Ann
page 67

Decodable Words
Target Skill: Long *i* Spelling Patterns
igh, y, ie
bright, by, cried, flight, fly, high, my, night, sighed, sky, tight, try

Previously Taught Skills
am, an, and, Ann, at, back, bat, best, Beth, bit, boasted, brown, buddy, bugs, can, can't, catch, cave, dark, far, feet, flew, free, from, gave, get, go, good, got, grasp, groaned, hanging, happy, held, help, helped, her, in, is, it, Jane, landed, large, last, let, let's, lift, liked, me, much, needed, net, new, odd, out, pick, safe, Sally, saw, she, smile, snagged, so, sound, sounds, spent, stiff, still, strong, thanked, that, then, this, time, took, tugged, up, will, wing, with, you

High-Frequency Words
New
across, cried, heard, large

Previously Taught
a, away, could, hear, hearing, I, of, said, the, they, to, was

Ty and Big Gilly
page 75

Decodable Words
Target Skill: Long *i* Spelling Patterns
igh, y, ie
bright, by, cried, fighting, fly, high, right, sight, sky, tried, try, Ty

Previously Taught Skills
and, as, at, back, baited, bed, best, big, biggest, bite, blue, box, bug, bugs, cast, clean, closed, dad, day, filled, fish, fishing, forth, gave, Gilly, glad, go, grabbed, had, happy, hard, he, head, hiked, him, his, hobby, hook, hooks, in, it, its, jelly, jumped, keep, kept, king, lake, landed, large, let, lid, liked, line, made, neat, off, on, out, pale, plop, reel, rod, sand, sat, snapped, sorts, still, stuff, sunny, swam, tail, that, that's, then, threw, time, took, under, up, used, waited, went, winked, with

High-Frequency Words
New
across, cried, head, large, second

Previously Taught
a, all, of, one, the, to, was, water, what

172

Bird Watching

page 83

Decodable Words

Target Skill: Base Words/Inflections
biggest, faster, fastest, flies, flying,
runner, shiniest, strongest, sweetest,
swimmer

Target Skill: Long *i* Spelling Patterns
igh, y, ie
bright, by, flies, flight, fly, flying, high,
might, right, sight, sky, spy, sunlight

Previously Taught Skills
24, and, as, at, best, big, bill, bird,
bird's, bird's, but, can, dive, down,
eggs, fan, few, fish, fit, flash, fun, has,
hawk, hen's, huge, hush, if, in, is, it,
its, keep, large, like, long, look, looks,
lot, low, nest, not, quite, race, racecar,
scoops, sea, see, sings, songs, swim,
tail, take, than, that, then, this, three,
too, up, which, you, zoom

High-Frequency Words

New
across, large

Previously Taught
a, are, do, eyes, hear, of,
one, open, the, to, want,
water, what, your

Benches

Decodable Words
Target Skill: Base Words/Inflections
beaches, benches, books, buddies,
cities, comics, couches, dads, dogs,
funnies, games, grown-ups, kids,
leashes, likes, lunchboxes, moms,
parks, pets, places, playing, puppies,
rains, reading, resting, sitting, streets,
towns, winners, yards

Target Skill: Long *i* Spelling Patterns
igh, y, ie
bright, by, might, sight

Previously Taught Skills
and, at, can, chat, city, dad, eat, flow,
for, go, good, in, is, it, jump, like,
lunchtime, me, not, on, or, out, outside,
play, read, rest, rope, sea, see, side, sit,
still, sunny, them, then, this, too, when,
win, you, zoo

High-Frequency Words
New
ball, should

Previously Taught
a, are, don't, have, I, many,
over, some, the, they, to,
watch, what

Quiz Game

page 99

Decodable Words

Target Skill: Suffixes *-ful*, *-ly*, *-y*
furry, helpful, hopeful, icy, loudly,
quickly, slowly, softly, spotty, squeaky,
stinky, sweetly

Previously Taught Skills
an, be, big, biggest, bird, black, book,
bright, by, can, cat, claws, did, dog, each,
feathers, fish, five, fly, for, fun, go, growl,
has, hump, I'm, in, is, it, leap, legs, like,
long, looks, make, me, more, new, page,
path, purr, quick, quiz, shell, sing, six,
snake, sound, stripes, swim, than, that,
this, three, took, which, white, wiggle,
will, you, you'll, zigzag, zip

High-Frequency Words
New
idea, minute, took

Previously Taught
a, animal, animals, are, do,
have, the, was, water

Jack and the Beans

Decodable Words

Target Skill: Suffixes *-ful, -ly, -y*
bagful, cupful, gladly, handful, hopeful,
hopefully, joyful, quickly, thankful

Previously Taught Skills

after, an, and, as, at, ate, back, bean,
beans, big, black, but, came, cow, did,
down, drenched, dry, dug, fat, feed,
feel, felt, fetch, food, for, get, good, got,
green, grew, had, happy, he, helped,
hill, his, in, it, Jack, Jack's, Jill, land, last,
liked, long, looked, lot, much, nice, not,
oatmeal, on, pail, picked, plan, planted,
plants, plot, rakes, rows, see, sells,
she, silly, soil, soon, spades, sprouted,
sprouts, still, such, that, them, then,
those, time, took, town, traded, up,
upset, waited, went, with

High-Frequency Words

New
beautiful, idea, listened,
thought, took

Previously Taught
a, could, have, of, one,
some, the, their, they, to,
was, water, were, would

Ruth's Day

Decodable Words

Target Skill: Long Vowel Spelling
Patterns: *a, e, i, o, u*
Edith, I, I'm, Ruth, Ruth's, she, so, table

Target Skill: Suffixes *-ful, -ly, -y*
chilly, Crunchy, funny, goofy, grateful,
loudly, quickly, sleepy, slowly, so, soggy,
squishy, sweetly

Previously Taught Skills

and, at, ate, back, bed, beeped, big,
book, bus, buzz, buzzed, came, class,
clock, day, did, down, dressed, felt, fun,
gave, get, got, grinned, had, happy, her,
hers, home, hug, in, it, it's, joke, just,
knock, know, last, late, left, let, like,
little, math, missed, Mom, not, on, or,
out, Pops, road, sat, she, sit, smiled, still,
stopped, stretched, that, them, time,
too, use, went, when, with, yawned

High-Frequency Words

New
caught, friendship

Previously Taught
a, great, have, of, said,
school, the, to, was, your

Stew for Peg

page 123

Decodable Words
Target Skill: Long Vowel Spelling
Patterns: *a, e, i, o, u*
able, be, cozy, he, hi, Hugo, I, Jo, Lulu, she, Toby

Target Skill: Suffixes *-ful, -ly, -y*
cupful, handful, helpful, loudly, quickly, really

Previously Taught Skills
an, and, ask, asked, back, big, birthday, by, came, chattered, did, didn't, for, green, had, happy, heat, help, helped, her, home, hooted, hot, how, in, is, it, it's, know, leaves, likes, make, must, not, on, Owl, own, Peg, Peg's, Pig's, pot, quacked, red, sat, smells, squealed, stew, stuff, such, thank, thanks, that, this, treat, up, went, will, with, you, yummy

High-Frequency Words
New
friendship, idea

Previously Taught
a, all, of, put, said, some, the, to, was, water, what, your

LESSON 30

Amy Ant

Decodable Words
Target Skill: Syllable Pattern (CV)
able, Amy, before, cozy, decides, music, over, reminds, returns, Rupert, tiger

Previously Taught Skills
after, and, Ant, as, at, back, backpack, be, bed, better, blooming, blue, brave, crawls, day, days, did, down, each, ending, feels, field, fills, flies, flower, flowers, flying, for, full, fun, get, go, good, happy, has, he, help, her, him, his, home, how, hums, is, it, its, last, leave, long, look, makes, mantis, meet, most, name, next, not, now, on, out, pick, room, roses, sad, saves, see, sees, she, shouts, sleepy, slides, slips, smell, sniffs, so, soon, spring, summer, sunny, sunshine, sweet, take, tells, thanks, that, time, too, tune, up, wakes, waves, way, when, will, winter

High-Frequency Words
New
field, loves, most

Previously Taught
a, are, been, come, every, full, have, hears, into, of, one, some, talk, the, they, to, walks, you're

Julie and Jason

page 139

Decodable Words
Target Skill: Syllable Pattern (CV)
able, baby, before, behave, behind,
believe, beyond, cozy, even, Jason, Julie,
Julie's, over, silent, table

Previously Taught Skills
after, an, and, as, asked, back, big, black,
by, can, cat, curls, day, did, dinner,
dog, drapes, each, eats, feeds, find,
for, fur, got, had, happy, has, hay, he,
her, hidden, hide, hides, him, his, hop,
hopped, house, hunts, hutch, if, in,
it, lap, let, like, likes, looked, missing,
named, no, not, off, on, or, out, outside,
pellets, pet, picnic, places, plant, play,
playing, porch, rabbit, sad, saw, see,
seek, seeks, seen, she, sit, sits, sleeps,
smiled, so, spotted, still, takes, them,
then, time, too, took, up, upset, when,
white, with

High-Frequency Words
New
brothers, everyone, sorry

Previously Taught
a, all, away, couldn't, idea,
of, one, the, they, to, was,
were

LESSON 30

Home at Last

Decodable Words

Target Skill: Prefixes *un-*, *re-*
repainted, replaced, unloaded, unpack, unpacked, unwrapped

Target Skill: Syllable Pattern (CV)
before, began, belonged, cozy, decide, over, repainted, replaced, table, Tony, Tony's

Previously Taught Skills
and, at, ate, bed, bedroom, blue, books, box, brighter, but, came, chose, Dad, day, did, dishes, felt, first, found, glad, happy, he, helped, his, home, in, it, let, lights, like, liked, long, look, looked, lot, made, meal, Mom, much, new, nice, noon, old, paint, pans, pots, quickly, room, set, settle, sheets, so, started, still, then, things, three, toys, up, van, which

High-Frequency Words

New
everyone, loved

Previously Taught
a, do, family, of, put, the, their, there, they, to, was, were, where, workers

181

Soccer

page 155

Decodable Words

Target Skill: Prefixes *un-, re-*
react, replaying, retelling, unkind,
unlike, unsafe, unskilled

Target Skill: Syllable Pattern (CV)
behave, believe, decided, over, remind

Previously Taught Skills

and, at, be, best, blue, boys, bump, by,
can, catch, chose, coach, coach's, dots,
dressed, each, ends, fast, feet, field,
first, for, from, fun, game, games, get,
girls, goal, goalkeeper, goalkeepers,
goals, good, has, he, her, his, is, it, job,
keep, kick, kids, kind, long, look, made,
making, matter, may, more, most, must,
need, no, on, or, out, pads, pick, play,
player, players, plays, red, safely, same,
say, score, she, shin, shirt, shirts, skillful,
skills, soccer, socks, sport, stop, stripes,
teach, team, teams, team's, telling,
these, this, tries, try, up, using, when,
wins, with

High-Frequency Words

New
everyone, field, most, only,
people

Previously Taught
a, are, ball, have, into, many,
of, putting, the, their, to,
who

182